The Depository
Trust Company

The Depository Trust Company

DTC's Formative Years
and Creation of
The Depository Trust &
Clearing Corporation (DTCC)

William T. Dentzer, Jr.

YBK Publishers
New York

YBK Publishers, Inc.
39 Crosby St.
New York, NY 10013
www.ybkpublishers.com

ISBN 978-0-9800508-5-1

Library of Congress Control Number: 2008937270

Manufactured in the United States of America

Ver 8-10

Contents

Preface

This book describes the development and formative years of The Depository Trust Company (DTC), a period stretching from the late 1960s to the mid-1990s. It tells how conditions that regularly forced the New York Stock Exchange to shut down after 8 million share–trading days were changed to permit share-trading days in the billions as a routine matter.

The book is not a comprehensive history of DTC during this period. It is rather a description of major developments and strategies in the depository's evolution through my eyes as chairman and chief executive officer from 1972 until my retirement 22 years later. I set out not just to establish and grow DTC but also to get the "big things" right—company culture, governance, and efficient responsiveness to users.

At the turn of the century, after the period covered by this book, DTC became the core of what is now The Depository Trust & Clearing Corporation (DTCC). Then, several securities clearing corporations were consolidated with DTC. Because of differences in each company's membership, rules, and financial liabilities, each company, including DTC, became subsidiaries of a new holding company, DTCC. The book's epilogue considers this and other developments through yearend 2007.

Introduction

This history tells how Wall Street, paralyzed by post-trade paperwork in the 1960s, developed the largest and most efficient trade settlement system in the world, capable of handling billions of shares and dollars daily.

It recounts how financial industry leaders in New York worked across parochial industry boundaries in the early 1970s to create the basis for DTC and build a path for progress that reached across America.

It illuminates the unglamorous "plumbing" that links Wall Street back offices and the events that occur after a securities trade—the process known as trade clearance and settlement through which buyers gain ownership of securities and sellers receive payment.

It reports how continuous automation of the new depository's internal systems and its communications links with banks, broker-dealers, and clearing agencies across the country led increasingly to lower costs, greater accuracy, and fail-safe performance.

It tells how DTC developed essentially as a high-class cooperative whose duties were to absorb processing tasks from users, meet user needs, and operate at cost—refunding to users all revenues not needed for its operation.

It explains why DTC is not chiefly a holder of securities in safe custody, but rather an automated bookkeeping system providing multiple services leading to, or stemming from, the custody of securities.

It documents DTC's growth through 1994, the year of my retirement, when it processed, *inter alia*, $34 trillion in book-entry securities deliveries, $404 billion of cash dividend and interest payments, and $662 billion in underwritings, with securities valued at $7.7 trillion on deposit at yearend.

It records how, beginning in 1999, several clearing corporations were consolidated with DTC to create The Depository Trust & Clearing Corporation (DTCC), whose settlement systems processed $1.86 quadrillion of securities transactions and payments during the year 2007.

Through this history, you will come to know a national asset of which few are aware. You will learn also why, when stock in your brokerage account is donated to favorite charities, the stock is delivered to the charities' accounts through DTC.

The Depository
Trust Company

Chapter 1

BASIC's Seminal Role

It took a financial crisis to bring together the disparate, competing and often warring parties in New York's financial industry to address solutions to the "paperwork crisis" of the 1960s. It then took the skillful leadership of a few banking and securities industry leaders to lay the groundwork for DTC and set the path it should follow.

At its peak, the paperwork crisis caused the post-trade processing of securities transactions valued at hundreds of millions of dollars to be delayed or to fail entirely, dividends to investors to be misdirected, and brokerage firms to go bust. As the volume of investor purchases and sales rose, brokers' back offices were swamped. Stock certificates had to be received from sellers and sent to transfer agents for cancellation and issuance of new certificates in the names of buyers as required for proof of legal ownership. As a result, transfer agents were swamped, too, causing long delays in the provision of new certificates to brokers for their clients. The agents, typically banks, blamed brokers for the chaos and the brokers blamed the banks. Both were partly right.

For years, various industry committees and consultants had addressed the problems caused by rising trading volume. In 1962, the New York Stock Exchange led an effort across the United States to amend Article 8 of the Uniform Commercial Code to enable the transfer of ownership and pledge of securities by depository book-entry, as well as by the delivery of physical certificates.

However, it was not until the Banking and Securities Industry Committee (BASIC) was formed in March 1970 that real progress began to occur. The Depression-era Glass-Steagall Act that had separated commercial and investment banking since 1933 was still in place, and both industries doubted each other's competence. Never before had both industries tackled interindustry operational problems jointly at the most senior level. BASIC's members were:

John M. Meyer Jr., Committee Chairman
Chairman, Morgan Guaranty Trust Company

Herman W. Bevis, Executive Director
Retired Senior Partner, Price Waterhouse & Co.

Robert W. Haack, President, New York Stock Exchange, succeeded by James J. Needham in September 1972

William H. Moore, Chairman, Bankers Trust Co.

Ralph S. Saul, President, American Stock Exchange, succeeded by Paul Kolton in June 1971

Richard B. Walbert, President, National Association of Securities Dealers, succeeded by Gordon S. Macklin in April 1970

Walter B. Wriston, Chairman, First National City Bank

For two years, BASIC and its staff carefully gathered facts, analyzed previous studies, developed standardized forms to replace conflicting forms used by various industry groups, testified in Congressional hearings, and evaluated the solutions offered by different advocates. Its most important recommendation was to immobilize stock certificates in a comprehensive national securities depository system that included banks as well as broker-dealers, and to create that depository in New York. The depository would be built on the fledgling Central Certificate Service (CCS), a division of the NYSE Stock Clearing Corporation.

The functions of Stock Clearing Corporation were to compare and verify trade data input from brokers, issue delivery instructions, and complete trade settlement—the point where buyers of stocks pay sellers and become owners. Settlement could occur by book-entry delivery against payment when brokers had deposited stock for that delivery into their CCS accounts. The NYSE activated CCS in 1966, first accepting only limited deposits of the securities held by its member brokers, and then, in 1968, encouraging book-entry deliveries from those securities positions on deposit. Those deliveries met with mixed results initially but were considered successful by 1970.

BASIC's plan was that CCS be spun out of the NYSE and established as an independent, self-supporting interindustry company with a bank charter. The member banks of the New York Clearing House would then deposit their vast holdings of securities with the depository and henceforth use it, confident that they would be represented on its board of directors by right as stockholders, not at the sufferance of the NYSE. Banks, as fiduciaries and custodians, held billions of dollars of securities, including billions owned by mutual funds and insurance companies. Bank participation in the depository therefore would immobilize these securities and vastly expand the number of book-entry deliveries effected on and reported by the depository's computers, replacing the cumbersome transportation and presentation of certificates accompanied by paper instructions through the chain of parties involved.

The driving forces in BASIC were John Meyer, Herman Bevis, and Walter Wriston. They were motivated not only by public spirit and a sense of responsibilty as industry leaders, but also by concern that the U.S. Congress would impose a governmental solution to the problems that would prove tardy, inefficient, and inadequate. They also wanted the securities depository to have a bank charter so that it would be regulated, at least in part, by one or more bank regulatory agencies and subject to annual bank examinations; this would give banks greater confidence in surrendering the

John M. Meyer, Jr.
BASIC Chairman, 1970–1973
Chairman, Morgan Guaranty Trust Co.

Herman W. Bevis
BASIC Executive Director, 1970–1973
Retired Senior Partner, Price Waterhouse & Co.

huge volume of securities in their vaults to the care of the fledgling depository. Bankers generally considered broker-dealers in that era to be poor managers and sought ways to subject depository safeguards to external scrutiny.

To further entice banks to join and use the depository, an ownership formula was agreed upon which gave the banks a significant minority share of entitlement to depository stock and representation on its board of directors. This was part of a memorandum of understanding signed by the members of BASIC in September 1971.

BASIC also was active during this period in support of modifying state laws across the country that limited a depository's ownership so that the New York depository's user-ownership principle could be implemented.

BASIC was active in Washington, D.C. as well in trying to shape developing Congressional legislation that would give the Federal Reserve System a role in the regulation of securities depositories along with the Securities and Exchange Commission. These efforts eventually succeeded, as reported later.[1]

---

1 For further information see *BASIC—Interindustry Teamwork,* Banking and Securities Industry Committee, April 1, 1974. Library of Congress Catalog Number: 74-82905

Chapter 2

Transition to DTC

The first step in implementing BASIC's plan for the new depository was to select its chairman and chief executive officer.

Not long after I announced my intention to resign as New York State Superintendent of Banks, the state's chief bank regulator, John Meyer, and Herman Bevis approached me about heading the depository. We had met on several occasions while I was superintendent. Since they had been unable to get the Federal Reserve or the Comptroller of the Currency to consider chartering the proposed depository, they wished to have it chartered as a New York limited-purpose trust company. BASIC's lawyers believed such status was necessary so that the depository could serve as a "custodian bank" in a national depository system under the applicable section of the Uniform Commercial Code. I had told them I was willing in principle to issue a charter if the SEC desired it and if the commission would take the major role in regulating the company after it ceased to be an NYSE subsidiary subject to SEC jurisdiction. I did not believe the State Banking Department had the experience to adequately supervise such an enterprise.

In one of SEC Chairman William Casey's visits to New York, he encouraged me to charter the depository. Bill Casey was a colorful New York lawyer before President Nixon appointed him Chairman of the SEC. It was known that Casey had wanted instead to become director of Central Intelligence, a post he later assumed under President Reagan and where his propensity for borderline activity became more widely known.

After considering conflicting opinions on whether the proposed depository was the best vehicle to solve the post-trade processing problem, I agreed to let Meyer and Bevis propose my candidacy. I believe they proposed it largely because of my background, including a two-year public record as State bank regulator, and because I was not likely to be opposed by the constituencies involved. Many banks thought well of my regulatory tenure, though some felt otherwise; these mixed feelings may have helped assuage securities industry officials who might have opposed appointing a banker as CEO.

NYSE chief Bob Haack agreed to my appointment as chairman and CEO so long as the current operating chief of CCS, Diran Kaloostian, was named president and chief operating officer. Since at the time I knew nothing about securities clearance and settlement or the systems essential to the depository's operations, I was only too glad to oblige.

On June 1, 1972, I began the work of separating CCS from the NYSE Stock Clearing Corporation, developing the application for trust company status, and supporting the amendment of fiduciary, trust, and estate laws in many states that did not contemplate the existence of a securities depository. I also sought to influence pending Congressional legislation and draft the rules of the new depository for SEC approval. In all of this I greatly benefited from the wisdom of Herman Bevis and Thomas A. Williams, a brilliant lawyer at Milbank, Tweed, Hadley & McCloy who for many years served invaluably as the depository's outside counsel, attending all of its monthly board meetings.

To begin the separation process, CCS was incorporated in October, 1972 as Central Certificate Service Inc. (CCS Inc.), a subsidiary of the NYSE, with me as chairman and CEO and Kaloostian as president. Among the members of CCS Inc.'s board of directors were three senior bank officers; James J. Needham, who was the new NYSE chairman; and other NYSE officers. It was not long until Needham began to resent my efforts to get officers of broker-dealers to replace NYSE officers on the depository's board. I wanted that board to be composed of executives from depository users to the greatest extent possible, and answerable only to users.

Jim Needham had been an SEC commissioner prior to his election as NYSE chairman and had accompanied William Casey during one of his meetings with me. After I became head of the depository, I was told that Needham earlier had aspired to my post. As NYSE chairman, Needham considered keeping CCS Inc. from spinning out of the NYSE, but BASIC was still monitoring developments and the imperious Walter Wriston quickly squelched that idea.

CCS Inc. publications reported that at yearend 1972, more than one billion shares were on deposit with a value exceeding $50 billion, and the value of book-entry deliveries for the year exceeded $163 billion.

Chapter 3

Foundational Years

Transfer to DTC

U pon receipt of our charter as a limited purpose trust company, the business of Central Certificate Service, Inc. was transferred in May 1973 to The Depository Trust Company, the name I had recommended to the board. Soon thereafter DTC became a member of the Federal Reserve System. Our charter was limited in scope since DTC sought no powers to accept demand or savings deposits or make personal and commercial loans. We remained a wholly-owned subsidiary of the NYSE until such time as more state laws were amended to permit a depository to be owned by entities other than a national securities exchange or association. Consequently, the depository continued to be regulated by the SEC.

DTC's nearly 800-member staff was drawn almost entirely from CCS Inc. The great majority of them were clerical workers handling the flow of certificates into the depository, out to transfer agents, and back from agents for depository custody or availability to broker-dealers as needed. One important newcomer was Thomas J. Lee, who had been hired to develop the depository's information technology systems. CCS had been served by NYSE's computer systems, and there was wide agreement that DTC should develop and operate its own, independent IT capability. New departments for personnel, finance, general counsel, audit, and general services also had to be established.

Services and Growth

The shares eligible for depository services at that time were some 3,000 issues on the NYSE, American Stock Exchange, National Stock Exchange, and over-the-counter market. At that point major depository services in these issues to its Participants, as these users were termed in DTC's rules, were to:

- Receive deposits of certificates.
- Deliver securities on deposit by book-entry.
- Receive and pass along payment for those deliveries.
- Process book-entry pledges of securities to banks.
- Maintain custody of deposited securities.
- Give broker-dealers certificates in their accounts for physical delivery to banks that had not yet joined DTC.
- Arrange transfer of certificates into the names of broker-dealers' clients upon request.
- Pass along cash and stock dividend payments due owners.
- Pass on proxies to broker-dealers providing voting rights for their clients.

Stock certificates deposited into the depository were transferred promptly into DTC's nominee name, Cede & Co. (shorthand for Certificate Depository), so that dividend payments and voting rights could flow to DTC and through it to its Participants and on to the beneficial owners of those securities. For individual investors who left securities with broker-dealers "in street name," the street name became Cede & Co.

Our goals at the time were to expand the type of eligible issues to include corporate bonds, speed the adaptation of banks to the depository, and increase the automation of depository operations and communications with users. Above all, we sought to avoid a loss or failure which would discredit the concept of depository processing.

The year 1973 marked the first year banks began to use the depository for more than the receipt of loan collateral from brokers. By yearend, the conversion of bank operating systems was such that 12 New York City banks and nine banks located in other states had begun depositing securities in and using DTC. This allowed the depository to inaugurate a new service, the institutional delivery (ID) system, providing an electronic path for trade confirmation, comparison and delivery of institutional trades involving a broker-dealer, an institution and the institution's agent custodian bank.

DTC's annual report for 1973 noted its move to new quarters at 55 Water Street under leases previously arranged by the NYSE and recounted the depository's growth to yearend: 4,729 eligible securities issues, 1.8 billion shares on deposit, $176 billion in book-entry deliveries, 32 million transactions, and 270 Participants.

One year later, in1974, DTC-eligible securities issues expanded by 34 percent to 6,356, more than two billion shares were on deposit as bank participation grew, and the first of several electronic communication systems was offered to users to replace the transport of paper instructions to the depository.

On the operations front, DTC in 1974 proposed a major change regarding stock transfer agents that allowed the depository to reduce its costs and risk. Under this plan, DTC would give back to a qualified transfer agent some or all of the certificates the agent had transferred into the depository's nominee name and sent to DTC for custody; thereafter, the agent would issue certificates to DTC only upon notice from the depository based on instructions from its Participants. This process allowed DTC to reduce the number of certificates in its vault, decreasing risk and reducing certificate-handling costs. In later years this procedure led to many transfer agents holding a single "balance certificate" that recorded DTC's fluctuating holdings of a security. Twenty years later, a number of those agents that had become highly automated held $4 trillion of such certificates on behalf of DTC.

Policies on Fees and Revenues

A foundational policy inaugurated in 1974 was to base DTC service fees on service costs. I anticipated incessant arguments with our disparate group of users if DTC's fee schedule was not based on objective grounds. We then began the first of what became annual studies of service costs led initially by our external auditor, Price Waterhouse, estimating direct and allocated costs for each service. Each year, the estimates of allocated costs—the most debatable element of cost and often the most intellectually difficult to allocate—became more refined.

With reasonable estimates of service volumes factored in for the year ahead, a fee was established for each service to be paid by all users, big or small. Users would pay only for transactions in the services, or type of services, they used. If service volumes were less than budgeted, temporary surcharges could be added. After yearend, excess revenues arising from higher-than-budgeted service volumes would be refunded to users *pro rata* based on the total of fees they paid to the depository. Cost-based fees were rigorously pursued. If some users desired a new service that other users did not need, that service would be developed and its development cost added to the initial service fee until that cost had been recovered.

Another fundamental policy decision was not to pay dividends to stockholders. BASIC had viewed user purchase of depository stock as a means to participate in DTC's governance and not as an investment vehicle, but had suggested paying a limited dividend. Even that, however, would require DTC to retain income in order to pay dividends and to pay taxes on that income. It would benefit users, though not the NYSE, to give users refunds of all excess revenues. After reimbursing the NYSE from DTC revenues for CCS's pre-1972 start-up expenses, that became our policy.

In December 1974, DTC announced its policy "to limit its profits and return to its users such revenues as the Board of Directors believe exceed the funds required for the depository's operation." After adding a half million dollars to surplus to build reserves, the depository returned $2.4 million to users—about 10 percent of its total expenses for the year.

Congress Acts

The year 1975 brought final passage of Congressional legislation affecting a securities depository after four years of consideration and lobbying. As favored by BASIC's members, the New York Clearing House Association, the Securities Industry Association and DTC, the Senate version of the legislation prevailed in conference over the House version. As a result, while the SEC was given primary responsibility for regulation of depositories, the Federal Reserve was given responsibility with respect to their safeguards for securities and funds. With this legislation—the Securities Act Amendments of 1975—bank fears about the nature of depository regulation, well-founded or not, were put to rest.

Sale of DTC Stock

The year 1975 also brought the initial sale of DTC stock as envisioned under BASIC's plan. Enough states had modified their laws to make it possible for the NYSE to sell some of its 100 percent ownership. Bank Participants were offered entitlement to purchase depository stock based on BASIC's ownership formula defining depository usage. Since BASIC had contemplated that the NYSE, the American Stock Exchange (Amex), and the National Association of Securities Dealers (NASD) would own DTC stock on behalf of their member broker-dealers, the Amex and NASD also bought shares. The resulting ownership of DTC stock was: NYSE 61 percent, Amex and NASD eight percent each, and 21 banks with a total of 23 percent. The principle of user ownership had begun to be implemented.

After bank users of DTC had purchased stock, some broker-dealers saw no reason why they should not be able to do so also, instead of being represented by their self-regulatory agencies. While DTC paid no dividends, those firms wanted at least the right to purchase stock if and when they desired. I agreed with these brokers and through a friend at Merrill Lynch prompted Merrill Lynch chairman Donald Regan to propose action on this matter by the NYSE. Regan was a member of the NYSE Board (and later treasury secretary and White House chief of staff under President Reagan). I believed NYSE Chairman Needham would not want to fight Regan on this subject, which proved to be correct. Thus, after approval by the NYSE Board, broker-dealers became eligible to purchase DTC stock in 1976.

A Participant's entitlement to purchase DTC stock was based on its annual usage of the depository. Usage was defined by a formula devised by BASIC that gave equal weight to fees paid to the depository and the market value of long positions at DTC. The weight given to long positions was designed to ensure that banks, with their large holdings of securities but much less fee-generating activity than broker-dealers, would have more than very minor representation on the depository's board of directors.

Participants were not required to buy stock but could buy any or all of their stock entitlement prior to the stockholders meeting to elect directors. That election was by cumulative voting, which insured that holders of 51 percent of the stock could not elect all directors. Entitlement to purchase stock was calculated and offered annually so that a Participant that had not bought stock always knew that it and others could buy stock the following year if DTC's management and board were not deemed responsive to Participants.

In February 1977, 23 of 210 eligible broker-dealers bought 11.4 percent of DTC stock. The stock they did not purchase remained with their self-regulators, but the principle of user ownership and control had been firmly established. That spring DTC had 50 stockholders.

Chapter 4

Growth and More Growth

D TC's priorities were unchanged throughout the 1970s: increase the number and types of eligible securities; expand institutional use of the depository to widen the scope of book-entry trade settlements; speed automation of internal depository functions to reduce clerical errors and headcount; automate more communication links with users; and design new services in close cooperation with industry committees. To support the latter, we began publishing periodic program agendas describing the depository's plans for the coming year and beyond so that users could react and proceed with their own complementary automation planning.

While banks were depositing securities into DTC, many of their large institutional customers—insurance companies, pension funds, and mutual funds—could not permit their custodian banks to deposit their securities as well. Securities owned by insurance companies, for example, by state law had to be held within the state in which the insurance company was chartered. State laws and regulations across the country had to be changed.

In a multi-year effort, DTC enlisted regulatory agencies, legal bodies, industry associations, and others to make these changes, with growing success in the late 1970s. The depository also assisted

17

efforts by its participating banks to educate their correspondent banks and other institutional customers about the benefits and safeguards for their securities.

Until these legal barriers were removed, DTC had to keep many certificates on deposit in its Cede & Co. nominee name available for "urgent withdrawal" on several hours notice from Participants needing to deliver physical certificates to agents for institutional buyers not yet allowed to have them in DTC. These certificates had to be in the correct denominations as well, e.g., 35,700 shares. Periods of sustained high trading volume put especial pressure on our work force, requiring continuous daily mandatory overtime to process the flood of these urgent withdrawals.

To reduce one major cause for certificate withdrawals, DTC developed an automated voluntary offerings service in 1977. Participants with the right to surrender securities for cash and/or other securities to agents could then exercise that right without having to withdraw certificates themselves for presentation to agents. Instead, Participants exercised their rights by using the depository as the vehicle for communicating with agents for those offers. The next year, DTC inaugurated a service for the distribution of initial public offerings (IPOs) and other underwritings by book-entry to make it unnecessary for transfer agents to create, underwriters to distribute, and other Participants to process certificates soon destined for deposit at DTC.

The number of eligible issues expanded greatly in 1978 with the addition of 2,400 over-the-counter issues. This accommodated the 1977 merger of the clearing corporations of the NYSE, the American Stock Exchange, and the NASD that formed the National Securities Clearing Corporation (NSCC). This merger centralized the clearance and settlement of broker-to-broker trades and made NSCC an intimate partner of DTC, which acted on NSCC instructions to deliver securities to and from NSCC member broker-dealers' DTC accounts.

Table 1 depicts the remarkable growth in the volume of some major DTC services and other metrics in its first ten years and in the ten-year period thereafter.

Table 1

	1973	1983	1993
Eligible Securities Issues	4,739	70,397	1,154,897
Book-entry Deliveries (market value)	$176 billion	$3.57 trillion	$27.8 trillion
Securities on Deposit (yearend value)	$9 billion	$1.24 trillion	$7.54 trillion
Participants (yearend)	270	475	515
Annual Expenses	$22,423,000	$107,101,000	$297,659,000
Full-time Staff (yearend)	832	2,066	2,609

Source: DTC Annual Reports

Apart from its major services to users were others of cost-saving importance to them. For example, DTC acquired information on corporate actions, such as dividend record and payable dates, that users could rely on the depository to provide rather than gathering such data themselves. They also could use DTC as a vehicle for reclaiming taxes that had been improperly withheld by foreign tax authorities rather than pursuing reclaims themselves.

The chapters that follow consider important aspects of DTC's further development by subject area, rather than treating them in a chronological account.

Chapter 5

Expanding the Number of Eligible Securities

E xpanding the number and types of securities issues eligible for DTC's cost-saving services was a continuing priority of the depository and its users, particularly broker-dealers who dealt with a wide range of issues.

As mentioned earlier, a total of 3,000 NYSE, American Stock Exchange, National Stock Exchange and over-the-counter (OTC) issues were eligible at yearend 1973, the first year of DTC's existence.

When the depository first made corporate bonds eligible in the mid-1970s in response to user requests, it ran right into a textbook chicken-or-egg dilemma stemming from a new service offering involving physical certificates: A given user wanted book-entry services but also wanted DTC to have a critical mass of securities already on deposit before depositing its own securities. This made new service start-ups difficult.

In the case of corporate bonds, newly deposited bonds had to go to trustees after action by transfer agents. This delayed DTC's receipt of bonds registered in its nominee name that Participants might need for urgent withdrawal of certificates to present to buyers' agents who could not yet accept book-entry delivery. Participants, therefore, had to be persuaded to accept some early processing pain in order to reach the longer-term pleasure of cost-saving, automated operations for everyone.

A major expansion of OTC issues began in 1978, with 2,400 issues added, and more followed in subsequent years. Broker-dealers needed this expansion since they traded such issues, but banks largely did not; further, since there were fewer certificates in shipments to most OTC issue transfer agents and hence fewer DTC-billable items, the banks could end up subsidizing this issue expansion. This problem was resolved by following the depository's cost-based fee policy and establishing a "less active issue" surcharge for certificate-related services in any securities issue, not just OTC issues, below a certain level of items.

The expansion of OTC issues caused major operational problems. To put it mildly, a number of the additional transfer agents with which DTC had to interact were not as professional as agents for larger companies. Many hundreds of OTC companies acted as the transfer agent for their securities, and some were accustomed to charging for the issuance of new certificates. When one such agent was contacted about its delayed processing, a youthful voice responded that dad and mother were off on vacation. By yearend 1980, a total of 14,233 issues were DTC-eligible, an increase of more than 11,000 since 1973.

An even greater expansion of eligible issues began in 1981 when DTC undertook to immobilize outstanding bearer, registered, and interchangeable municipal bonds and offer distribution of new issues through underwritings. Not long thereafter, to capture unreported interest income on bearer bonds and to thwart criminal use of bearer bonds to launder money, the U.S. Congress adopted legislation requiring tax-exempt bonds for maturities of more than one year to be issued only in registered form, beginning in 1983.

Making bearer municipal bonds eligible for deposit into DTC entailed new risks, since any "bearer" could convert them into cash. These unusual risks required special controls. One such control measure was a unique vault built on Long Island that ultimately housed some 22 million bearer certificates, each with a face value of $5,000. Each year, 44 million coupons—one per certificate in the customary six-month cycle—were clipped and shipped to paying agents to receive bond interest due for Participants.[2] A plethora of paying agents and, later, transfer agents for registered issues, often were themselves the issuers—e.g., a Mississippi sewer district. This created an abundance of processing problems for DTC. Only DTC's certificate level control—its numerical record of every certificate entering its vaults—enabled it eventually to overcome disputes with many of these agents about their performance. In total, DTC's records contained the names and addresses of some 5,000 agents.

The depository's municipals program gained speed after Congress set its 1983 deadline, and it revolutionized the nature of muni issuance and processing. Issuers of municipal securities were used to paying one-time printing costs of bearer bond certificates; they were not eager to pay transfer agents for repeated issuances of registered certificates in serial and term bonds, each of which was defined as a separate issue with its identifying CUSIP number.[3] Broker-dealer underwriters and DTC pitched the depository's ten-year record of book-entry accomplishment to these issuers, and new issues increasingly were distributed through DTC. The year 1982 saw the first of many "book-entry-only" underwritings with no certificates available to investors; investors' ownership instead was reflected on the periodic statements received from their brokers or other financial intermediaries.

At yearend 1983, more than 48,000 municipal issues were eligible. They were joined by almost 23,000 issues of common and

---

2   The passage of time saw this vast number of bearer bonds dwindle as these issues matured or were called by issuers. This vault was closed early in the new century.

3   The term CUSIP derives from the 1964 standard for identifying securities issues developed by the Committee on Uniform Security Identification Procedures (CUSIP), formed by the American Bankers Association. The standard was not widely used by banks and broker-dealers, however, until BASIC pushed self-regulatory organizations such as the NYSE in the early 1970s to require its use.

preferred stock listed on various exchanges and OTC, corporate debt, U.S. Treasury and Federal Agencies, warrants, American Depository Receipts, unit investment trusts, and units, which combine two or more securities, such as a stock and a warrant. More issues in these types of securities were added in subsequent years, as well as new types such as 144A securities traded by qualified institutional investors and global securities that traded in the U.S. and other countries.

After making eligible new variations of some of these securities—e.g., stripped municipal bonds—and certificates of deposit (CDs) in book-entry-only form, DTC in 1987 began making eligible securities that settled only in same-day (Federal) funds. The depository's same-day funds settlement system (SDFS), designed like many other new services under the leadership of James V. Reilly, operated in tandem with its system for other securities that by industry practice settled in next-day (clearinghouse) funds. The new system afforded eligibility to municipal notes, zero coupon bonds backed by U.S. government securities, municipal variable-rate demand obligations, medium-term notes, collateralized mortgage obligations, auction-rate and tender-rate preferred stock and notes and certain types of government agency securities not eligible for the Federal Reserve's book-entry system.

The year 1990 saw the first issuance through SDFS of commercial paper—unsecured, unregistered, short-term promissory notes issued largely by major U.S. corporations. Developed, as usual, after extensive advice from industry committees and after review by the Federal Reserve and SEC, this service provided electronic issuance and settlement of commercial paper in book-entry-only form. At yearend 1991, one-third of all outstanding commercial paper—almost $177 billion—was on deposit at DTC. Late in 1992, the Federal Reserve removed its limit on the program's expansion after the depository demonstrated that its new backup data center could fully recover within three hours if disaster took down its primary data center. At yearend 1993, $409 billion was on deposit, 74 percent of all outstanding commercial paper.

Other money market instruments were made SDFS-eligible in 1994 including institutional certificates of deposit and municipal commercial paper, with bankers' acceptances due to follow after adoption of enabling amendments to the Uniform Commercial Code.

At yearend 1994, the year I retired, eligible securities issues numbered 1,193,404, a long way from 1973's 3,000 issues.

Shareholder Communications

While seeking to immobilize certificates, DTC sought also to avoid being a barrier between issuing companies and the beneficial owners of voting securities. A securities position listing was provided to all issuers of voting stock as of record date for their annual meetings and at other times upon request. This listing showed the number of shares held in DTC by any Participant. DTC then assigned all voting rights for stock registered in its Cede & Co. nominee name to those Participants, indicating the number of shares for which each was responsible and removing the depository from the chain of subsequent communications from issuers.

Chapter 6

Setting Industry Standards

TC's huge holdings of securities and attention to detail placed special pressure on paying agents, tender and exchange agents, transfer agents, and others in the business of servicing securities to meet high industry standards. Its dealings with agents for cash dividend and interest payments indicate the economics and politics involved.

Cash Dividend and Interest Payments

Since securities on deposit at DTC were registered in its Cede & Co. nominee name, the depository received cash dividend and interest payments to pass on to its Participant users. In 1973 it received $1.2 billion in such payments, many of them after the payable date and not in good (same-day or Federal) funds.

DTC began challenging corporations and their paying agents to meet the NYSE standard for listed companies: to make good funds available to investors on dividend and interest payable dates. Companies and their paying agents generally mailed checks to investors or their custodians and enjoyed the float until checks were cashed. Many protested that DTC was demanding special,

27

even discriminatory, treatment. We responded that the NYSE rule meant what it said, that we would happy to have messengers pick up checks at their offices, and that DTC bore responsibility to speed the proceeds through to its Participants. This effort, spearheaded by DTC Vice President Arnold Fleisig, who was responsible for this area and who had been a member of BASIC's staff, led to slow improvement.

In 1980, letters bearing my signature were sent to the CEOs of all companies in cases where they or their agents had failed to make timely payments to DTC on recent quarterly payable dates. The letters suggested that we might publicly identify their treatment of investors. One of these letters went to Raleigh Warner, chairman and CEO of Mobil Oil, who was also a member of the NYSE Board.

During this period NYSE President John Phelan was speaking at regional meetings of the American Society of Corporate Secretaries as he prepared to become chairman and CEO of the NYSE. Phelan was met with complaints about my letters at these meetings. Within the NYSE, Phelan let it be known that he was contemplating changing the NYSE rule. With on-time payments rising, I worked out a *modus vivendi* through an NYSE officer, subsequent Exchange head Richard Grasso, that I would refrain from citing the NYSE rule and that the rule would not be changed.

Another problem existed. DTC would receive some dividend and interest payments too late in the day to credit them to Participants' daily settlement accounts, and in any event could not do so in same-day funds in its settlement system geared to next-day (clearinghouse) funds. We could and did invest payments received in Federal funds overnight, however, and in 1980 began refunding these interest earnings to Participants in proportion to their share of such payments. Later, with the advent of our same-day funds settlement system, dividend and interest payments due Participants were credited in that system.

The substantial amount of annual cash dividend and interest payments processed by DTC is shown in Table 2 at 10-year intervals from 1973.

Table 2

1973	1983	1993
$1.2 billion	$54.8 billon	$401.1 billion

Source: *DTC annual reports*

Transfer Agents

Certain tensions lay beneath the surface in relations between transfer agents and DTC. After all, DTC was reducing their revenues, pressing them to complete transfers more quickly, pushing them to automate to stay in business, and showing report cards on their performance to their regulator, the SEC. Finally, after much information and encouragement from the depository, the SEC promulgated performance standards for transfer agents to improve the time required to complete routine transfers.

Chapter 7

Forming DTC's Culture

S tarting with a blank slate, DTC's leadership built a company culture as a service organization that was professional, cost conscious, risk conscious, objective, transparent, and responsive to its Participants but impartial as among them. How did this happen?

Personnel

The first rule for any organization is to hire good people, individuals with intelligence, ability and good values. The rule is applied subjectively, of course; I was once described as a person with such high hiring standards that "Dentzer wouldn't hire himself." While that was said chiefly in jest, it is accurate to say I believed that managers should strive to hire persons smarter and wiser than themselves.

The obverse of that rule is to remove those who don't meet the test of good, objective leadership. That is why I forced the resignation of Diran Kaloostian as president in October 1974, though by mutual agreement we described it as a voluntary resignation due to differences in management philosophy.

A talented early hire, in 1974, was William F. Jaenike, a former member of the BASIC staff who previously worked for the American Stock Exchange on trading floor automation. Bill rose steadily through the management retirement ranks of DTC, becoming, on my recommendation, president and chief operating officer in January 1992, and succeeding me as chairman and CEO in September 1994.

Another key hire was Conrad F. Ahrens as president and chief operating officer in 1979. After Kaloostian's departure in October 1974, I had acted as chief operating officer in addition to CEO, and the depository had grown too much for that to continue. Con came to us from Citibank where he was senior vice president for securities operations, and he had been deeply engaged in BASIC's effort to create the depository.

In the early 1980s, compensation levels at DTC had risen to the point where it was possible to attract other able persons to DTC's management.

I had observed that Wall Street overpaid itself at senior and high revenue-producing levels through bonus practices and that a "halo" effect reached down to the operations level. Fortunately, awareness had grown that DTC's senior managers were something more than back-office operations people. Among the recruits added to management were two from the staff of the Municipal Securities Rulemaking Board whom I had met after municipals were made eligible. They were Richard B. Nesson and Donald F. Donahue, who joined DTC in 1986. Nesson became general counsel and Donahue was promoted to successively higher positions in diverse disciplines until he became DTCC president and chief executive officer in 2006 and chairman and CEO in 2007.

These and other key additions to senior staff, such as Larry E. Thompson in to the general counsel's office in 1981, and able persons like Dennis J. Dirks, who had been with the depository since its exception, formed the senior management team that helped propagate the depository's culture. Dirks later became president and chief operating officer in 1998, serving in that position at DTC and DTCC until his retirement in 2003.

Practices Adopted

DTC, as I have described earlier, functioned in a culture of tight controls and record keeping. The need to reconcile our data daily with that of Participants and others in response to our output helped in that regard. It was, however, with mixed emotions that I learned that many Participants began to trust our data more than their own.

DTC's certificate-level control—its unique record of the number on each certificate that ever entered its vault, coupled with a microfilm image of that certificate—was a safeguard that some industry operatives initially thought unnecessary and unduly expensive. It paid off handsomely, however, resolving countless disputes with transfer agents. Examples abound. The depository proved many millions of dollars of unintentional underpayments of dividends and interest by paying agents over the years and recouped those funds for Participants.

This control also made it possible to identify certificate withdrawals by Participants for which DTC subsequently had received dividend and interest payments. These payments, totaling in the millions of dollars, would have escheated to the state but instead, after research, were provided to affected Participants.

Tight expense controls were enforced for their own merit and to show our Participants that a "utility," as many considered us, could nonetheless be frugal. Economy class air travel was prescribed, even for me, unless special circumstances were present. At a large gathering upon my retirement, Bill Jaenike noted, "(Dentzer) spent DTC's money as if it was his own."

Requests for charitable donations from DTC were treated in a similar vein. In New York City, funds typically are raised at charity dinners where corporations buy tables to demonstrate their social conscience and CEOs reward other CEOs for buying tables at dinners they had hosted. My response to such requests was to indicate that DTC operated essentially as a cooperative, refunding excess revenues to users. Thus it was DTC's users and not DTC who should make decisions on charitable contributions. We made exceptions to this rule when a prominent officer of a Participant was on an event's organizing committee; in such cases we would buy one ticket but not attend.

As a general practice, we shunned publicity. Once institutional buyers of securities had been made aware of the depository's capability, I reasoned that everyone who needed to know about us did know about us. DTC was not a public company, nor a retail business needing to advertise. It was rather a custodian holding many millions of securities certificates for intermediaries. While certificates registered in DTC's nominee name would be difficult to negotiate if stolen, that was not the case with bearer certificates.

Another reason for a low profile was to try to reduce the number of ambitious hackers who might try to penetrate the security of our automated systems. We took this threat seriously and repeatedly hired outside professionals to attempt such penetration.

Code of Ethics

I wrote and promulgated a DTC code of ethics and business conduct in 1982 to apply to every DTC employee. I deemed it useful, though not sufficient, since the Wall Street back office culture was male, sexist, and characterized by gift giving to lubricate the wheels of operational activity. The code prohibited all employees from accepting gifts valued at more than $50. It also emphasized the importance of not discriminating in favor of any Participant and keeping information about all Participants confidential. The document was distributed annually, and employees were asked each year to sign an acknowledgment that they had read and understood it. They also were required to see a videotaped presentation, introduced by me, that described the code and its importance.

Embezzlement Discovered

What started out as a crisis for the depository turned out to be a blessing in disguise.

Briefly: in 1983 we became aware that a stock loan finder bribed a DTC night-shift supervisor in the settlement department to make a fraudulent entry directing stock valued at $750,000 to a brokerage firm. This was part of a larger scam undertaken by the stock loan finder, involving bribes to and kickbacks from employees at various firms. DTC retrieved the stock with the cooperation of the brokerage firm concerned and ordered a joint investigation of its operational controls and employee actions by its independent auditor, Price Waterhouse, and its outside law firm, Milbank, Tweed. We later learned from the U.S. Attorney's office that beginning in 1981, in exchange for bribes, the supervisor had misdirected a number of fraudulent stock deliveries permitting interest-free use of Participants' securities by others in suspense accounts overnight or over weekends.

The Price Waterhouse-Milbank investigation cast a wide net and cost DTC $1.3 million. It led to tightening of a number of operational controls and the ouster of some middle managers who had accepted gifts or placed uncritical trust in their staffs. Most importantly, it sensitized depository employees to seductive external threats and caused the tightening of our code of ethics. Employees and Participants were notified that DTC's policy was to discourage any and all gifts from Participants and others to any DTC employee. Further, any DTC employee receiving a gift, gratuity, entertainment or payment of personal expenses at any time was required to report the details in writing. Failure to do so could result in being fired.

At a meeting with all senior and middle managers after the investigation had ended, I concluded my remarks as follows:

> What it comes down to is that DTC managers at all levels have to be more careful, more ethical, and more professional than

the standard of Wall Street back office business-as-usual. DTC's reputation and future is at stake. If DTC is to reach its potential, both nationally and functionally, and if you want to participate in that future, all managers of this company will have to leave behind the old Wall Street back office culture of petty gifts, petty favors, uncritical loyalties, cronyism, and cutting of ethical corners. Think on the lessons of these past months and go on to manage on a higher, a professional, level.

Union Contract Negotiations

When the depository was spun out of the NYSE in 1972, it carried with it more than 700 clerical employees of the NYSE Stock Clearing Corporation that were members of Local 153 of the Office and Professional Employees International Union (OPEIU), an AFL-CIO affiliate. Union contracts were negotiated for three-year periods with the managements of the NYSE, DTC, and the NYSE's data processing subsidiary, with the NYSE taking the lead in a multi-employer contract. Typically, contract talks were concluded after collective bargaining sessions, strike threats, final consultations among the three employers, and off-the-record talks with John Kelly, OPEIU President. In our early joint negotiations, I learned much from wise labor counsel at the law firm of Proskauer, Rose. I also decided that I wished to negotiate future contracts separately from the NYSE in order to contain contract costs, but found little support anywhere for my wish.

During negotiations on a new union contract in 1981, NYSE Chairman John Phelan was said to be open to a nine percent wage increase for each of three years. I called that number "prodigal" and refused to go along, now with the support of my board, dragging out a contract settlement for weeks. My primary purpose was to create enough discomfort that Phelan would be happy not to have DTC be a partner in future multi-employer negotiations. My strategy worked. After contract settlement, and with Phelan's approval, I notified OPEIU that DTC would bargain separately in the next contract negotiations due in 1984.

I approached the 1984 negotiations prepared for the worst. I knew from salary surveys that our wages for all but the lowest paid union employees were measurably above Wall Street back office wages and our benefits even more so. I had seen the American automobile industry negotiate union contracts that rendered it uncompetitive because managements were unwilling to have assembly lines shut down by a strike. I was determined that would not happen to DTC. I told our staff that since DTC existed to serve its users, if it incurred a strike and could not operate despite that strike, DTC did not deserve to exist.

Contract negotiations dragged on. DTC management made its final offer on June 24, 1985. That offer was rejected at a poorly attended union membership meeting where militants argued that DTC could not function during a strike and would quickly fold. Next morning the strike was on and so was our contingency plan. We immediately mobilized replacement workers from DTC management, brokerage firms, banks located outside New York, consultants, and temporary hires. Fortunately, several hundred union members overcame peer pressure and crossed the picket line to come to work.

Union chief John Kelly called me that morning to disclaim responsibility for the strike and urge resumption of contract talks. I refused. Kelly even had New York Congressman Charles Rangel phone me. Meanwhile, union members crossed the picket line in increasing numbers. I held out for more than two weeks, determined to demonstrate that strikes against DTC would fail. On July 11, we reached a tentative settlement that was overwhelmingly ratified by the union's membership, with contract provisions essentially identical to our earlier final offer. Those who struck lost almost three weeks' pay.

That was the end of serious strike threats to DTC. It also was the end of whispers from regional securities depositories that DTC's unionized labor costs would escalate out of control and that it could be disabled by a strike.

The period following the lengthy post-embezzlement investigation and the 1985 strike seemed to deepen employee understanding of DTC as a vital service organization and a good place to work. The depository's senior management group was in place, middle management was experienced, and training was offered to union members to improve job skills leading to advancement. Moreover, labor relations went smoothly under the attentive eye of deputy general counsel Larry Thompson, our most senior African-American executive, who was astute, fair, and approachable. The culture had been set and was deepening.

We used the three multi-year contracts following the 1985–1987 contract to make steady progress in containing the wage and benefit costs we had inherited from the NYSE. For example, the next contract sharply reduced retiree benefit costs and introduced employee premium-sharing for medical benefits. In 1990, employee medical premium sharing was increased and for two years of the contract, lump-sum payments took the place of general wage increases that would have had a compounding effect on future wage costs and salary-sensitive benefits. In the 1994 labor agreement, lump-sum payments in lieu of general wage increases were negotiated for the first three years of a five-year contract. In one of my letters to DTC employees explaining our final contract offer to the bargaining unit prior to its vote on the offer, I wrote:

> DTC's Participants know that DTC's clerical wages and benefits are higher and better than Wall Street pay and benefits for similar jobs. We view this wage offer as the best way to put money into the pockets of clerical employees while limiting increases in DTC's cost structure that, over the long term, make users less willing to choose DTC to provide new services.

Customer Satisfaction Surveys

What did DTC Participants think of the depository's overall performance in this period?

Annual surveys of Participant satisfaction with DTC signaled their satisfaction with its operation and, perhaps more importantly, showed depository management where improvements were needed. Since one of the most valuable elements of management is the objective evaluation of an organization's performance, these annual surveys of customer satisfaction served to improve future performance and underscore for our staff the importance of meeting user expectations.

Chapter 8

The DTC Board and Stock Ownership

T he NYSE owned 100 percent of the depository's stock until state law changes would permit broader stock ownership as agreed by BASIC's members. As a result, the initial annual elections of DTC's board of directors depended on the NYSE's implementation of BASIC's plan and my ability to influence the NYSE's choice of directors.

When DTC was formed in 1973, the New York Clearing House banks, as agreed by BASIC's plan, got three seats on the Board of Directors. Because bank directors would be a minority on a 15-person board—the size dictated by the N.Y. State banking law—the banks named high-level officers who carried weight, including Elliott Averett, President and CEO of The Bank of New York, and William I. Spencer, President of First National City Bank. Among others, the NYSE named George E. Doty, a General Partner at Goldman Sachs and John T. (Jack) Roche of Kidder Peabody. I was delighted because I wanted the rank and quality of board members to be high enough in their companies—executive vice president or higher—that they would be more likely to ignore parochial industry interests and deal objectively with issues where user interests did not overlap or were in conflict.

The procedure for annual director nominations, adopted on my recommendation, called for the nominating committee to make recommendations to the board, and for the board itself to make nominations to stockholders after giving Participants the right to make suggestions to the nominating committee. The nominating committee's recommendations to the board would include a report on any such suggestions. I considered it important for the full board to know of such suggestions and whether proposed candidacies might imply reservations about DTC management.

Jack Roche and others understood the importance of selecting board members from the securities industry who would see beyond narrow loyalties and be persuasive with other board members in overcoming industry parochialisms. The board accepted my recommendation that Roche chair its nominating committee. As Jack prepared to leave the board in 1980, he took me to meet Robert Baldwin, chairman and CEO of Morgan Stanley and chairman at the time of the Securities Industry Association, to explain our need for a top-flight candidate. That is how Richard B. Fisher, who later became Morgan Stanley's chairman and CEO, came to be a DTC board member from 1980 to 1984.

Successive DTC boards were at a high level of quality and rank within their companies. Some persons were sought out to become members; some were suggested by their superiors, probably for a mix of reasons; and some volunteered, also probably for a mix of reasons. Whatever their provenance, I believed that difficult issues explained objectively in papers distributed in advance of board meetings, to allow for thorough review by directors' staffs, would lead to board approval of management's recommendations. Sometimes it took back-to-back monthly board meetings to work through controversial subjects, but I was never disappointed.

Among outstanding board members in subsequent years were some who chaired board committees: Arthur F. Ryan of Chase Manhattan Bank, 1982–1986 (later chairman and CEO of

Prudential Financial), Thomas C. Schneider, executive vice president of Dean Witter Discover, 1983-1994, and Richard S. Pechter, president and CEO of DLJ Financial Services, 1985–1996. The nominating committee in my final year was an example of board strength; chaired by Tom Schneider, its other members were Dick Pechter, Jill M. Considine, president of the New York Clearing House Association, and H. J. (Jack) Runnion, Jr., senior executive vice president of Wachovia Bank of North Carolina.

Other subsequently prominent persons who served on the DTC board at one time or another are: Arthur Levitt Jr. in 1976 as president of Shearson Hayden Stone (later SEC chairman from 1993 to 2001); Richard Grasso, 1989–1993, as NYSE president (later NYSE chairman and CEO); John Thain of Goldman Sachs, 1994–1999 (later chairman and CEO of the NYSE in 2003 and of Merrill Lynch in 2007); and Richard G. (Rick) Ketchum, 1992–1998, as NASD executive vice president (later non-executive chairman of the Financial Industry Regulatory Authority).

Since all members of DTC's board were elected at annual meetings of DTC stockholders and not all users were stockholders, some general understandings had to be reached with large stockholders to accompany the text of the stockholders agreement and stock entitlement formula.

The stockholders agreement provided for an annual reallocation of entitlement to purchase depository stock by Participants or their representatives based on a formula that defined annual usage of the depository in the prior year. That formula was based equally on fees paid to the depository and the average market value of long positions at DTC as calculated on the last business day of each month. All purchases and sales of DTC stock were at book value per share at the end of the calendar year.

Participants were not required to buy stock. All New York Clearing House banks bought stock in 1975 per the BASIC agreement as did some banks outside New York that had become Participants. Some broker-dealers bought a portion or all of their stock entitlements when they were able to do so in 1976, but the great majority did not purchase for one or more of the following reasons: the stock paid no dividends; they were satisfied with DTC; they were more interested in the right to purchase stock than in exercising that right; and they could always buy stock the following year.

This pattern of limited stock purchases by Participants persisted for years, leaving the bulk of voting stock with its original sole owner, the NYSE. To its great credit, the NYSE reduced its number of board seats to one beginning in 1976, allowing more officers of broker-dealers to have board seats. It also always voted its stock for every candidate the DTC board recommended.

But the ownership formula eventually created another problem. The usage formula's award of equal weight to long-position market value and fees paid to DTC had been BASIC's contrivance to give banks more than a small minority of DTC board representation. BASIC knew that broker-dealers would pay the great bulk of depository fees since there were many more of them and they individually would have more activity because of the nature of their business. Walter Wriston acknowledged the weakness of parity in this formula when BASIC adopted it, stating that the formula could be reconsidered later if it created problems.

Yet when in 1981 I suggested reducing the weight given to long positions in the ownership formula, Wriston rebuffed me. The undue weight given to long positions in the formula had given New York banks entitlement to four board seats, up from three, and could generate more bank seats later. Wriston did not consider that a problem.

After being stymied then, I forged a consensus several years later that modified the ownership formula by reducing the weight of long-position market value in two stages: to 40 percent in 1987 and to 20 percent in 1988, with correspondingly greater weight given to fees paid to the depository.

I later won DTC board agreement that in its nominations for election of directors by stockholders, broker-dealers (including their representatives) would have seven seats and banks (including their representatives) six seats, with two seats reserved for DTC's chairman and its president. Later, we reached another consensus on the distribution of bank directors: three from New York and three from outside New York. Those results remained in place for the rest of my tenure.

Chapter 9

Investors and Their Certificates

In the days before DTC, and even during its early years, it was common practice for individual investors to have stocks they had purchased registered in certificates carrying their names. This was proof of ownership and protection against the possible insolvency or liquidation of their brokers. While these certificates could at times be forgotten, misplaced, or even stolen, the standard legal advice investors received was to have and hold certificates registered in their names, possibly in safe deposit boxes.

Upon sale of that stock, the certificates would be provided to brokers with an accompanying stock power, endorsed to the investor's broker. When brokers began to use DTC, they would deposit those certificates into DTC; DTC then would forward them promptly to transfer agents to assure they were "good transfer," i.e., not counterfeit, and registered into its Cede & Co. nominee name.

Purchases by investors who desired certificates registered in their own or other names led to millions of "withdrawal by transfer" instructions each year to the depository from its Participants. DTC would forward these instructions to the appropriate transfer agents, who would send new certificates to the depository for transmission to Participants and onward to the requesting owners.

DTC annual reports show the eventual decline in the number of these investor requests for certificates as broker-dealers became better capitalized and investors more comfortable about leaving their investments in "street name." While market booms and busts influenced the total annual number of certificates requested, Table 3 below depicts their gradual downward trend over 20 years.

To speed certificates to investors who desired them, DTC began a direct mail program in the mid-1980s that allowed transfer agents to mail new certificates directly to investors. The depository received registration data on investors from Participants by automated means and forwarded these data to agents in machine-readable form. If agents chose not to develop the automated capability required to mail certificates, DTC upon request would mail the certificates itself.

For many years, broker-dealers were reluctant to charge their investors for the costs of handling requests for certificates, fearing a competitive disadvantage with non-charging brokers. This began to change in the late 1980s, however, and charges for such a service increased in later years.

The downward trend in the number of certificates issued to investors accelerated in the early 1990s as more companies and their transfer agents allowed investors to register their ownership of company stock on company books; investors received statements from companies permitting such registration but received no certificates. This direct registration service was linked to DTC so that no certificate needed to be created when investors sold their stock.

Table 3

1976-1984	Certificates ranged from 8.8 to 11.7 million annually
1985-1987	Certificates ranged from 7.0 to 8.3 million annually
1988-1993	Certificates ranged from 4.8 to 5.7 million annually
1994-1995	Certificates ranged from 2.6 to 3.5 million annually

Source: *DTC annual reports*

A combination of a slimmer, more financially-sound brokerage industry, adaptation to a depository environment, increased investor comfort with automation, company desire to stay close to investors, financial disincentives to acquire certificates, and generational change had made the stock certificate an increasingly endangered species.

Chapter 10

What Happened to the "National System"?

B ASIC'S work in the early 1970s inspired interest in other U.S. financial centers, and BASIC assumed that a comprehensive national securities depository system would evolve with the New York depository linked to others in those centers.

The existence of other stock exchanges and their clearing corporations and of major banks in their cities that competed with New York banks caused the formation of the following securities depositories: Midwest Securities Trust Company (MSTC) in Chicago; Pacific Securities Depository Trust Company (PSDTC) in San Francisco; New England Depository Trust Company in Boston; and the Philadelphia Depository Trust Co. (Philadep) in Philadelphia.

DTC linked with all of them since broker-dealers needed to deliver securities in one depository to users of another depository. DTC was apprehensive about other depositories' weakness, however, and feared that a failure to settle an interdepository delivery of securities would trigger a financial loss to DTC. Moreover, there were continuing arguments, never resolved by the SEC, about whether interdepository interface fees to each other would be appropriate.

Given DTC's low fees due to its huge transaction volume and the widespread preference of banks headquartered outside New York to use DTC, it was only a matter of time until regional exchanges tired of losing money on their depositories and saw that DTC would not place them at a competitive disadvantage to the NYSE and other objectionable New Yorkers.

The Boston Stock Exchange folded the New England depository into DTC in 1981, and the PSDTC was absorbed at the request of the Pacific Stock Exchange beginning in 1987. Later, at the request of their respective exchanges, DTC absorbed the Midwest Securities Trust Company in 1995 and Philadep in 1997.

I thought throughout these years that as much as I despised monopolies, a DTC monopoly would be benign. Why? After all, monopolies tend to raise fees to customers unduly, let products or services slide in quality and ignore developing services for small customers. DTC, however, based its fees on service costs and operated on a not-for-profit basis; moreover, its user Board of Directors would fire management if services declined or did not meet user needs. Finally, the SEC had to approve every proposed DTC policy or service and would hear any complaint if the DTC Board was not responsive or tolerated unacceptable behavior.

Chapter 11

Perils and Challenges

Peak Days

The depository increased its computing power from time to time to insure it could process unanticipated high trading volume. While trade settlement occurred five business days after trade date (T+5), that five-day gap did not provide sufficient time to make changes to accommodate unusually high volumes.

When the market crash occurred on "Black Monday," October 19, 1987, the Dow Jones Industrial Average fell 22.6 percent and trading exploded for several days. Some questioned whether DTC could handle those volumes up to and including settlement day. They were handled without delay or incident, however, and for the first time DTC's systems processed over one million updates to Participant accounts on a single day.

Dealing With Failures To Settle

When deliveries of securities against payment were made, DTC sought to insure that buyers paid sellers under a "no ticket, no laundry" approach. DTC did not guarantee payment to sellers, however. The depository confronted its first failure to settle in 1973 when Weiss Securities failed to pay for securities delivered to its account. We then "reversed" the affected deliveries, returning them to their would-be deliverers so they would not lose their securities and could sell them out in the open market. Deliverers outside of a depository environment could lose both payment for their securities and their securities as well.

On May 18, 1982, Drysdale Securities Corporation posed a similar problem, unable to pay us its $4.5 million debit. After contemplating another reversal of deliveries, we held off final settlement while we negotiated successfully with Drysdale for rights, guarantees, and indemnities which allowed us to complete settlement and avoid a possible lawsuit for putting them out of business.

On a few other occasions, we reversed several deliveries to a Participant that was unable to pay its settlement obligations, returning to that Participant's counterparties the least number of deliveries needed to avoid a loss. We would do so only as a last resort and only after working well into the night with the Participant and its certifying bank.

A potential major crisis was averted in early 1990 when a sudden meltdown of a major brokerage firm, Drexel Burnham, was converted into an orderly termination of its business, thanks to the guiding hand of the Federal Reserve Bank of New York and its president, E. Gerald Corrigan. In addition to serving as vice-chairman of the Federal Open Market Committee, the president of the New York Fed is always the government's go-to man in financial crises. That is why, regardless of formal procedures, no one assumes that position without the approval of the chairman of the Federal Reserve Board. Corrigan pulled all the major players in the Drexel drama together so we all knew how the firm would be wound down and no one would start a stampede for the exit.

Business Continuity Measures/ Disaster Recovery

As DTC became more important to the securities industry, it became increasingly necessary to have back-up capabilities ready for emergencies. An early step, in 1981, was to have an emergency generator installed behind its 55 Water Street offices to provide power in the event of prolonged outages by Con Edison. In 1987, DTC's back-up data center began operation in Brooklyn with sources of electricity and telephone lines separate from those serving 55 Water Street. Later, data stored in DTC's back-up system was updated in real time and kept current with those in DTC's Water Street system.

International

As trading expanded across national borders, DTC began assessing its future role in international trade clearance and settlement. It developed an international institutional delivery (IID) system in 1990 to assist the clearance of institutional trades involving a foreign security or one or more counterparties outside the U.S. In 1993, it hosted the second international conference of central securities depositories in New York. Also in 1993, the German national depository became DTC's first international Participant, and DTC prepared to open an office in London to better serve its Participants' European operations. In 1994, agreement was reached on a draft amendment to the Uniform Commercial Code which, when adopted by the various states, would permit DTC to use a foreign custodian. While the depository did not anticipate its international role as becoming significant in the near future, it sought to fill service gaps where useful and to understand developing service needs for its services internationally.

Group of Thirty Report

In 1989 the prestigious international Group of Thirty (G-30), which included Citibank chairman and CEO John Reed, issued a report urging higher standards of trade clearance and settlement in major markets. Among other things, it called for shortening the

U.S. trade settlement period to three business days (T+3) from five (T+5) and to settle all trades in same-day, not next-day (clearing-house) funds. Enactment of these recommendations in the United States would lessen risk since the period of unsettled trades would be reduced along with overnight credit exposure. Unfortunately, enactment by 1992—in just three years—was proposed, a time frame that was quite unrealistic.

I had two problems with these recommendations, the burden of whose implementation would fall chiefly on DTC.

First, the G-30 U.S. working group proposed that the United States should "move to a certificate-less society by 1992." This was viewed as essential to achieving T+3 in that time frame, While there was widespread holding of physical certificates by individual investors, by 1992 investors would no longer be able to obtain certificates. Some thought the SEC would make this possible, but I knew from my dealings with Congress that this was a state law matter that Congress would not disturb. I did not want DTC associated with that recommendation since when the politics of it exploded, the first to be injured would be the depository and not a faceless working group.

Second, the G-30 working group's timetable was too short to move all settlements by 1992 to both T+3 and same day funds, even building on our present same-day funds settlement system. I knew G-30 was pressing the bright and forceful SEC Chairman, Richard Breeden, to endorse that early timetable, and I feared that he might.

Therefore, when DTC was asked to join the working group on implementing the G-30 recommendations, I declined to do so with the full backing of the DTC board of directors. My June 8, 1989, letter to that effect set off a storm. I later told working group chairman Lewis Bernard of Morgan Stanley that DTC would join the group if it would drop the proposal to abolish the stock certificate, but that proposal was not dropped.

At an SEC-sponsored roundtable discussion on the G-30 recommendations in 1990, I was chided for not supporting those proposals by a message from New York Fed president Corrigan delivered by his representative. At the same meeting, SEC chairman Breeden, in response to a newspaper article, disclaimed any notion that the SEC would abolish the stock certificate. That meant early conversion to the T+3 date was not possible, that Breeden would not be stampeded, and that work could go forward on implementing T+3 and same-day funds settlement on a reasonable schedule.

After redesigning a number of systems and mounting a massive campaign to educate thousands of users and their clients about the many changes required, DTC led and implemented seamless transitions to T+3 in June, 1995, and to same-day funds settlement in February, 1996. With the latter, bank Participants anywhere in the United States could settle their DTC accounts through the Fed wire, instead of through New York clearing house banks.

DTC's new settlement system prevented a Participant's failure to settle by requiring all Participants to have cash or other collateral in their accounts at all times sufficient to offset debits entering their accounts. At the end of each business day, after netting all credits and debits, a Participant would be in either a net credit or net debit position, that is, due to receive payment from or make payment to, the depository. The existence of the Participant's collateral assured its payment.

Chapter 12

Retirement Day

I retired on September 1, 1994, having reached DTC's mandatory retirement age of 65 for senior officers. I had put that limit in place years earlier when one senior officer wished to stay on beyond that age. I wanted our able younger officers who might be wooed away to know that the old ones would not stay on indefinitely and that there would be room at the top. When it became my turn to retire, I left the depository in the good hands of the two persons I had recommended: Bill Jaenike became chairman and CEO and Tom Williams president.[4]

At yearend 1994, DTC Participants numbered 501: 335 broker-dealers, 157 banks, and nine clearing agencies. The user ownership principle was well established with 140 stockholders: 59 broker-dealers, 75 banks, and six self-regulatory organizations and clearing agencies. Since Participants were not required to purchase any or all of their annual entitlements to stock, the NYSE still held 34.6 percent, with the NASD and Amex holding smaller amounts. DTC's full-time employees numbered 2,542 and its expense budget for the year was just over $300 million.

---

4 Jaenike served as chairman and CEO until January 1999, when he was succeeded by Jill Considine. Sadly, Tom Williams died of a heart attack in the spring of 1998 after more than 25 years of wise counsel to DTC and other clients during his 31 years of corporate law practice.

Securities immobilization had reached a high level. At yearend 1994, DTC held in custody for its Participants 72 percent of NYSE-listed company shares, 58 percent of the shares of issues in the NASDAQ stock market, 50 percent of American Stock Exchange-listed issues, 89 percent of the principal amount of outstanding corporate debt listed on the NYSE, and 95 percent of the outstanding principal amount of municipal bonds.

More importantly, DTC offered Participants a wide range of automated services for those securities with a company culture oriented to serve all of those competing users equally—banks and broker-dealers, large and small, institutional and retail, money center and regional.

Just as the operations of the regional securities depositories had been and were still being absorbed into DTC as I retired, I expected future consolidation into DTC based on industry recognition of the depository's competence, culture and capability. This included the Participants Trust Company, which processed and held Government National Mortgage Association (Ginnie Mae) securities—folded into DTC in the late 1990s—and eventually NSCC and its related companies.

Beyond those foreseeable events and the expansion of the depository's international activity, I believed that the future of DTC would see major developments that no one then could predict. Less than a decade later, that had proved to be the case (see Epilogue).

At an industry retirement dinner in my honor at the New York Hilton, I expressed confidence that DTC would continue its high level of service to diverse users and my happiness in the job now concluded. I ended my remarks quoting an ancient Greek adage, "Happiness lies in the exercise of vital powers, along lines of excellence, in a life affording them scope." Then with a smile to my knowledgeable audience, I added, "I am not certain that the field of clearance and settlement normally offers as much scope as one might desire, but the timing of my watch and its challenges made it so for me."

William T. Dentzer, Jr.
DTC Chairman and CEO, 1973–1994

Conrad F. Ahrens
DTC President, 1979–1992

William F. Jaenike
DTC President, 1992–1994
DTC Chairman and CEO, 1994–1999

Thomas A. Williams
DTC President, 1994–1998

Dennis J. Dirks
DTC President, 1998–1999
DTCC President, 1999–2003

Jill M. Considine
DTC Chairman and CEO, 1999
DTCC Chairman and CEO, 1999–2006, Chairman, 2007

Donald F. Donahue
DTCC President, 2003–2006, CEO, 2006
DTCC Chairman and CEO, 2007

DTC's 25th Anniversary Celebration

Chairman and CEO Bill Jaenike celebrated DTC's 25th anniversary in 1998 from the rostrum overlooking the NYSE floor. From left to right the speakers are SEC Chairman Arthur Levitt, NYSE Chairman and CEO Richard Grasso, former NASD Chairman Gordon Macklin, Jaenike, former chairman of First National City Bank (later Citigroup) Walter Wriston, and Bill Dentzer. Macklin and Wriston in 1970–73 were members of BASIC, the interindustry committee that spawned DTC.

Bill Dentzer, DTC's first chairman and CEO, addresses the speakers before addressing the audience.

SEC Chairman Arthur Levitt addresses the audience.

Former Citigroup chairman and CEO Walter Wriston addresses the audience.

Epilogue

T wo major developments affecting the depository occurred around the turn of the century. One was the consolidation, beginning in 1999, of the clearance and settlement of U.S. corporate and municipal securities in an entity based largely on DTC. The second was the impact of the September 11, 2001 attacks on the World Trade Center, an event requiring new safeguards for the future functioning of U.S. capital markets.

Until the consolidation mentioned above, NSCC and DTC were sister companies headquartered in the same building, 55 Water Street in lower Manhattan. NSCC operated a clearance and settlement system for broker-to-broker trades that was a major source of instructions to DTC to move securities between brokers' DTC accounts on settlement day. NSCC offered other services to broker-dealers as well, including programs for stock loans, customer account transfers between firms, and mutual fund purchases and sales. NSCC, however, was essentially a product development and marketing company whose computing and operations were administered by the Securities Industry Automation Corporation (SIAC) and, to a small extent, by DTC.[5] DTC, on the other hand,

---

5 SIAC was formed in 1972 to assume the computing and automation tasks of the NYSE and the American Stock Exchange. The NYSE owned two-thirds of SIAC stock and the Amex one third. Since SIAC processed the work of the NYSE and Amex clearing corporations before they merged to form NSCC, SIAC assumed the

was an operating company and an order of magnitude larger than NSCC.

In the late 1990s, when Bill Jaenike was DTC chairman and CEO, a consensus grew among participants in both DTC and NSCC that NSCC and its related clearing corporations should be integrated with DTC in a manner that respected their similar, though not identical, membership and differing rules and financial liabilities. During 1999, The Depository Trust & Clearing Corporation (DTCC) was formed as a holding company, with DTC and NSCC becoming its subsidiaries and Jill M. Considine DTCC chairman and CEO. Considine, a DTC board member since 1993, had succeeded Jaenike as the depository's chairman and CEO upon Jaenike's retirement in January 1999. The integration of these two companies proceeded under her leadership thereafter.

Later (in 2002), as previously planned, the Government Securities Clearing Corporation and the Mortgage Backed Securities Clearing Corporation became DTCC subsidiaries as a step toward their emergence in 2003 as the Fixed Income Clearing Corporation (FICC).

As the third major DTCC subsidiary, FICC provided trade comparison and settlement services for various Ginnie Mae, Fannie Mae, and Freddie Mac mortgage-backed securities and for certain transactions in eligible U.S. Treasury bills, notes, bonds and zero-coupon securities as well as book-entry non-mortgage-backed Federal Agency issues.

Other DTCC subsidiaries subsequently formed were DTCC Deriv/SERV, providing automated post-trade matching services for over-the-counter derivatives including credit default swaps, equity derivatives and interest rate derivatives; and Global Asset Solutions, supplying global corporate action validation services to

---

same processing duties for NSCC and the functions NSSC later absorbed from the National Clearing Corporation of the NASD.

financial intermediaries. By then, DTCC also owned 50 percent of Omgeo, a joint venture with Thompson Financial Inc. providing post-trade pre-settlement services to investment managers, broker-dealers and custodians in the U.S. and foreign countries.

DTCC thus became a holding company for a group of subsidiaries and a joint venture that provides the critical infrastructure for the clearance and settlement of securities transactions in the U.S. and related services to participants in the financial markets. While the DTCC board of directors also serves as the board of each subsidiary, each subsidiary is a separate legal entity with its own rules and is not responsible for the obligations or liabilities of the others.

The impact of the World Trade Center attack was to underscore the importance of business continuity in the face of disasters that could shut down major American securities markets.

As the devastating tragedy unfolded in lower Manhattan on 9/11, DTCC processing fell back seamlessly to its backup data center in Brooklyn, across the East River from its 55 Water Street data center, and kept operating there until communications links in the Wall Street area were restored. Thereafter, since a future disaster affecting a broader area of New York City now seemed possible, the SEC and Federal Reserve required DTCC to build backup sites in remote locations and to take other measures to insure business continuity in any emergency. When DTCC later absorbed the processing of NSCC and FICC functions previously performed by SIAC, backup arrangements became more tightly integrated.

All of these developments, along with user desires that DTCC expand its capabilities in order to reduce financial firms' costs and risks, produced a DTCC that is now larger and more complex than the sum of its former parts at the time of their consolidation.

DTCC's 2007 volumes of activity in key services, after annual expenses of about $692 million, illustrate its present scope:

- Processed an average of 54 million transactions each business day with a single day high of 99 million.

- Settled book-entry deliveries of securities, including money market instruments, with a value of $364 trillion.
- Received and passed through to users $3.8 billion in cash, dividend, interest, redemption, and reorganization payments.
- Held custody at yearend of securities valued at over $40 trillion in 3.5 million issues.
- Distributed underwritings of 54,266 initial public offerings valued at nearly $4.3 trillion.
- Processed $2.5 million in mutual fund transactions for over 1,000 fund families and broker-dealers.
- Processed almost $21 billion in the value of annuities and other insurance products, premiums, and commission payments.
- Matched and confirmed transactions in credit, interest rate, and equity OTC derivatives for almost 1,100 institutions reaching over 90 percent of trades in credit default swaps (CDS), and launched an automated central repository where information in CDS contracts can be tracked over their life cycle.

In addition, Omgeo, DTCC's joint venture with Thomson, served more than 6,000 investment managers, broker-dealers and custodian banks in 42 countries. Its volume of U.S. trade confirmations in 2007 surpassed 350 million, and it matched more than one million domestic and cross-border trade confirmations monthly. Since almost half of DTCC's users are firms that are international in scope, this service and others scheduled for launch in 2008 respond to user wishes for less costly means to clear, settle, and manage custody of foreign securities.

Information on all DTCC services can be found on its website at www.DTCC.com.

Like its forbears, DTCC is an organization that operates at cost, seeking not profit but reduction of user costs and risks and refunding excess revenues to users. DTCC also operates on the principle of user ownership. The DTCC stockholders agreement requires any full-service user of DTC, NSCC, or FICC to purchase its entitlement to DTCC stock and permits certain limited and foreign securities depository users to do so as well. Because the NYSE and NASD owned NSCC at the time of its integration into DTCC, the stockholders agreement also allows both entities to vote for one director at the annual election of DTCC's Board of Directors, which currently numbers 21 members.

As with DTC's earlier stock entitlement formula, a user's entitlement to purchase DTCC stock is based 80 percent on fees paid to DTC, NSCC, and FICC in the period since the last stock reallocation and 20 percent on the average market value of that user's securities on deposit at DTC as of the last business day of the month during that period. Stockholders vote their shares at the annual election of DTCC's Board of Directors. At yearend 2007, DTCC common stockholders numbered 381.

Also in 2007 and culminating her succession plan, Jill Considine retired as DTCC chairman and was succeeded by Don Donahue, who had been named its chief executive officer the previous year.

Bibliography

BASIC-Interindustry Teamwork, Banking and Securities Industry Committee, April 1, 1974. Library of Congress Catalog Number: 74-82905.

Annual Reports of The Depository Trust Company, 1973–1998.

Quarter Century of Trust, A Short History of The Depository Trust Company, The Depository Trust Company, 1998.

Annual Reports of The Depository Trust & Clearing Corporation, 1999–2007.

Index

Author's Notes

I wish to thank DTCC for permitting me to reprint photographs of officers that appeared in DTC and DTCC annual reports. I also wish to thank Bill Jaenike, my successor as DTC chairman and CEO, for his helpful comments on a draft of this book and for photos taken at DTC's 25th Anniversary celebration.

About the Author

William T. Dentzer, Jr. was chairman of the board and chief executive officer of the depository for 22 years, from June, 1972 until September, 1994. Prior to that he served two years as New York State Superintendent of Banks after a year as executive director of the N. Y. State Council of Economic Advisers.

Before coming to New York in 1969, he held various senior U.S. government posts concerned with international economic development. His last assignment in Washington was as deputy U.S. representative, with the personal rank of Ambassador, to the Organization of American States and the Council of the Alliance for Progress. Prior to that he was director of the U.S. Agency for International Development mission in Peru.

www.ingramcontent.com/pod-product-compliance
Lightning Source LLC
Chambersburg PA
CBHW071111210326
41519CB00020B/6257